WILD ABOUT SNAKES

ANACONDAS

BY MEGAN KOPP

Consultant:
Robert Mason, PhD
Professor of Zoology
J.C. Braly Curator of Vertebrates
Oregon State University, Corvallis

CAPSTONE PRESS
a capstone imprint

Edge Books are published by Capstone Press,
151 Good Counsel Drive, P.O. Box 669, Mankato, Minnesota 56002.
www.capstonepub.com

Books published by Capstone Press are manufactured with paper
containing at least 10 percent post-consumer waste.

Library of Congress Cataloging-in-Publication Data
Kopp, Megan.
    Anacondas / by Megan Kopp.
    p. cm.—(Edge books. Wild about snakes)
    Includes bibliographical references and index.
    Summary: "Describes anacondas including their distinctive
characteristics, habitats, and defenses"—Provided by publisher.
    ISBN 978-1-4296-5432-6 (library binding)
    ISBN 978-1-4296-6255-0 (paperback)
    1. Anaconda—Juvenile literature. I. Title.
QL666.O63K67 2011
597.96'7—dc22   2010027375

Editorial Credits
Kathryn Clay and Anthony Wacholtz, editors; Kyle Grenz, designer;
    Eric Gohl, media researcher; Eric Manske, production specialist

Photo Credits
123RF/Benjamin Gelman, 1
Alamy/James Cresswell, 16–17; Mladen Curakovic, 18; Peter Arnold,
    Inc., 28–29; Steven J. Kazlowski, 22–23; vario images GmbH &
    Co.KG, 6–7, 12–13
Dreamstime/Colette6, 15; Martin Krause, 9
Getty Images Inc./AFP/Ishara S. Kodikara, 21
Minden Pictures/Ingo Arndt, cover
Photo Researchers, Inc/Tom McHugh, 14
Photolibrary/Morales Morales, 20; Peter Arnold/Nick Gordon, 4–5;
    Peter Arnold/Roland Seitre, 26–27; Peter Arnold/Tony Crocetta, 27
    (right); Tony Crocetta, 25
Shutterstock/Dr. Morley Read, 10–11; malko, 13 (person silhouette);
    Marilyn Volan, background; Paunovic, 13 (snake silhouette)

Printed in the United States of America in Stevens Point, Wisconsin.
042011   006196R

TABLE OF CONTENTS

ON THE HUNT   4

SIZING UP
ANACONDAS   12

SURVIVING
IN THE WILD   20

PROTECTING
ANACONDAS   24

Glossary..........................30

Chapter 1

ON THE HUNT

A slight rustle comes from the bushes in a forest. A giant otter stops walking and stands on alert. Moments pass and the bushes stop moving. Once again the otter begins walking. Out of the corner of its eye, the otter spies the head of an anaconda.

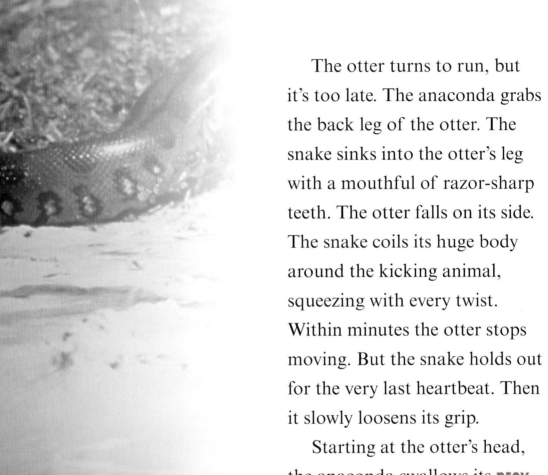

The otter turns to run, but it's too late. The anaconda grabs the back leg of the otter. The snake sinks into the otter's leg with a mouthful of razor-sharp teeth. The otter falls on its side. The snake coils its huge body around the kicking animal, squeezing with every twist. Within minutes the otter stops moving. But the snake holds out for the very last heartbeat. Then it slowly loosens its grip.

Starting at the otter's head, the anaconda swallows its **prey** whole. With a swollen belly, the snake rests. It won't need to hunt again for weeks.

prey—an animal hunted by another animal for food

Legless Lizards

Anacondas are not as developed as other snake species. Instead, these **reptiles** share many traits with crocodiles and lizards. In fact, anacondas are sometimes called legless lizards. Thousands of years ago, anacondas had legs. Although they no longer have legs, they do have spurs attached to what remains of their pelvis. The spurs and pelvis are leftovers of what were once legs and hips. Boas and pythons have similar spurs.

Like all reptiles, anacondas are **cold-blooded**. Their bodies are the same temperature as their environment. Anacondas use heat from the sun, water, and rocks to keep their bodies warm. When anacondas get too cold, their giant bodies move slower than usual.

reptile—a cold-blooded animal that breathes air and has a backbone; most reptiles lay eggs and have scaly skin

cold-blooded—having a body temperature that changes with the surroundings

7

In for the Kill

Anacondas are lay-and-wait **predators**. Rather than actively hunt for food, they prefer to hang out at the bottom of shallow water. They hide among the plants and wait for food to come to them. Moving their giant bodies to search for food would take too much energy.

When prey comes nearby, anacondas grab it with their mouths. These giant snakes have almost 100 sharp teeth, all pointing backward. The teeth hold the prey in place while the snake wraps its thick body around the animal.

Next, the anaconda **constricts** its prey. The snake squeezes until the prey can no longer breathe. When the prey stops moving, the snake uncoils its body and swallows the animal whole in one big gulp.

Anacondas digest their food slowly. After a large meal, they may live an entire year without eating again.

predator—an animal that hunts other animals for food

Big Mouth

Like many snakes, anacondas can eat very large animals. Some people think they do this by unhinging their jaws to get their mouths around the prey. But this is a myth. Most **vertebrates** have jawbones that are fused together. But anacondas don't have this type of jawbone. Instead, anacondas have elastic skin and tissue that stretches around large prey. Without a breastbone, their bodies can change shape as a large animal is swallowed.

Anacondas cannot hear and have poor eyesight. To find prey, they feel for vibrations on the ground or in water. Anacondas can also find nearby prey by smell. They flick their long, forked tongues in and out. The tongue catches smells and places them on the roof of the snake's mouth. This area is called Jacobson's organ. The organ lets the snake know if prey is nearby.

Anacondas are not picky about what is on the menu. Like all snakes, they are **carnivores**. They eat everything from birds and turtles to full-grown deer. Despite spending so much time in the water, anacondas rarely eat fish. Some people think that this slow-moving snake is no match for a fast fish.

vertebrate—an animal that has a backbone
carnivore—an animal that eats only meat

Chapter 2

SIZING UP ANACONDAS

Anacondas are some of the longest snakes in the world. Only reticulated pythons are longer. Most snakes range from 1 to 6.6 feet (.3 to 2 meters) in length. But female anacondas can stretch up to 28 feet (8.5 m). Male anacondas are much smaller. They are only about one-fifth the size of females.

Anacondas are not just long. They're heavy too. Most wild anacondas weigh between 200 and 300 pounds (90 and 136 kilograms). Some scientists estimate that a large female can weigh up to 550 pounds (250 kg). That's more than an adult lion!

The average height of an American male is 5 feet, 10 inches (178 centimeters)

Water Snakes

Anacondas are members of the Boidae family, which also includes boa constrictors and pythons. Members of this family are all non-**venomous** and pose little danger to humans.

venomous–able to produce a toxic substance

Most boas live on land, but anacondas prefer slow-moving, muddy water. The water helps support the large snake's heavy weight. In fact, anacondas are often called water boas because they spend so much time in the water. Their bodies are perfectly suited for a life underwater. Their eyes and nostrils are located near the tops of their heads. The snakes are able to see and breathe while swimming. Anacondas are also able to hold their breath for long periods of time.

Green Anacondas

When people talk about anacondas, they are usually referring to the green anaconda species. Also known as the common anaconda, the green anaconda is the heaviest snake in the world. These snakes live in South American rain forests near the Amazon River and on the Caribbean island of Trinidad.

The green anaconda has a red-brown stripe on its head. Black oval spots cover its olive-green body. This pattern of spots helps **camouflage** the snake. Like all anacondas, green anacondas also have a unique pattern of scales on the bottom of their tails. Much like a human fingerprint, the pattern can be used to identify individual snakes.

camouflage—to hide by using coloring that makes an

Beyond Green

Most information about anacondas comes from studying green anacondas. But there are three other species of anacondas. They are the yellow anaconda, the DeSchauensee's anaconda, and the Bolivian anaconda.

The yellow anaconda looks similar to the green anaconda. It has white, dark brown, or black spots on a yellow or green-yellow body. These snakes are not as large as their green relatives. A yellow anaconda reaches an average length of about 10 feet (3 m). Yellow anacondas are found in southern Brazil, Paraguay, eastern Bolivia, Uruguay, and northern Argentina.

yellow anaconda

North America

Europe

Asia

Africa

South America

Australia

Antarctica

N
W E
S

The DeSchauensee's anaconda was named after the person who discovered it in 1924. Also called the dark-spotted anaconda, this species looks similar to the yellow anaconda. They are found on Marajo Island and in parts of nearby Brazil. These snakes are quite rare, so few scientists have studied them.

The Bolivian anaconda was first discovered in 2002 along the Beni River in Bolivia. These snakes have dark spots and scale patterns shaped like rings.

Chapter 3

SURVIVING IN THE WILD

Anacondas mate once each year in the spring. Females ready to breed give off a scent to attract males. Several males fight each other for the chance to mate with a single female. This mating process may take as long as four weeks. Six months later, the babies are born.

Producing Young

Carrying the weight of so many babies can be difficult for pregnant anacondas. To reduce their weight, the snakes often don't eat during their entire pregnancy. They also remain mostly inactive. To help the babies grow, female anacondas come out of the water to lie in the sun. The warmth of the sun helps raise their body temperatures.

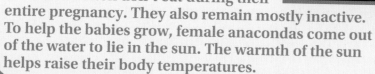

While many snakes hatch from eggs, anacondas are born live. Females usually give birth to 20 to 40 babies at one time. Some anacondas have had as many as 70 babies at one time. Babies are about 2 feet (0.6 m) long at birth. As soon as they are born, the babies are able to swim and hunt for food. They also face many dangers. About half of all baby anacondas are eaten within their first year by birds, jaguars, and other snakes.

Growing Up

Baby anacondas that survive their first year grow quickly. In just three years, they can reach up to 10 feet (3 m) long. At this point, they are fully grown and ready to mate.

Because of their size, adult anacondas have only a few predators. They must watch out for small alligators called caimans and humans who hunt them for their skin. Some people capture the snakes to sell to zoos or as pets.

Anacondas can live for more than 28 years in zoos and 15 years in the wild.

Anacondas and People

Despite their size, anacondas are not a major threat to humans. These snakes don't hunt animals they cannot swallow, and most humans are too large to eat. However, anacondas are easily angered. They may bite people trying to handle them. Though anacondas are non-venomous, their sharp teeth can cause serious injury.

Chapter 4

PROTECTING ANACONDAS

Anacondas are difficult to study because they hide so well. Little was known about these snakes until 1992. That's when the Wildlife Conservation Society and the Venezuelan Wildlife Department began studying anacondas in their natural habitats. These groups hoped to learn more about anacondas in order to better protect the snakes.

During part of the study, several anacondas were fed radio **transmitters**. The 6-inch (15-centimeter) units were built to last eight months. The transmitters allowed researchers to follow the snakes' movements and gather information about the snakes' habitats.

transmitter—a device that sends out radio signals

Snake Scientist

Jesús Rivas has spent many hours searching for anacondas on the Venezuelan plains. Trudging through the mud, he's well aware of the dangers that exist. Besides angry anacondas, there are caimans, piranhas, freshwater stingrays, and fire ants.

Rivas often walks barefoot when searching for anacondas. He says it's the best way to feel for snakes among the plant roots. When he finds an anaconda, he must get control of the head before the snake bites. The snake usually tires and stops fighting within 15 minutes. Rivas then covers the snake's snout with a cotton sock, which is gently taped to keep the jaws closed.

Catching the snakes is only one part of the project. Blood samples are taken from the captured snakes. The snakes' markings are examined, and their measurements are taken. Scales are clipped along the sides in a pattern that can be used for identification.

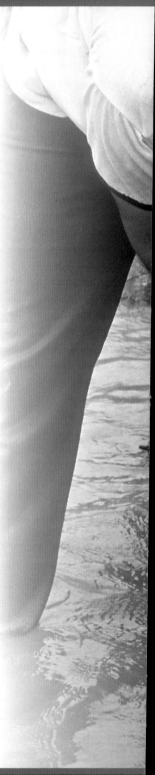

A Perfect Place to Study

The Venezuelan plains are a great place to study anacondas. During the rainy season, the plains flood. But for much of the year, the area is dry. During the dry season, anacondas are easily found and captured for study.

Since he began this study in 1992, Rivas has captured more than 1,100 adults and 300 baby anacondas.

Anaconda Survival

Anacondas play an important role in keeping the **ecosystem** healthy and balanced. Though these snakes are not endangered, they must still be protected. In most South American countries, it is illegal to hunt anacondas for their skin. But **poaching** remains a problem. People also move into anacondas' habitats and push the snakes out.

Many anacondas are simply killed out of fear. Because of their massive size, it's easy to understand why people would fear these snakes. It doesn't help that they're often shown as deadly, man-eating predators in movies. But it's important to remember that these snakes rarely attack humans, especially when left alone.

ecosystem—a group of animals and plants that work together with their surroundings

poach—to hunt or fish illegally

29

GLOSSARY

camouflage (KA-muh-flahzh)—to hide by using coloring that makes an animal look like its surroundings

carnivore (KAHR-nuh-vohr)—an animal that eats only meat

cold-blooded (KOHLD-BLUH-duhd)—having a body temperature that changes with the surroundings

constrict (kuhn-STRIKT)—to squeeze; anacondas kill their prey by squeezing it until it can no longer breathe

ecosystem (EE-koh-sis-tuhm)—a group of animals and plants that work together with their surroundings

endangered (in-DAYN-juhrd)—at risk of dying out

pelvis (PEL-viss)—the area of an animal that includes the hip bones

poach (POHCH)—to hunt or fish illegally

prey (PRAY)—an animal hunted by another animal for food

reptile (REP-tile)—a cold-blooded animal that breathes air and has a backbone; most reptiles lay eggs and have scaly skin

species (SPEE-sheez)—a specific type of animal or plant

transmitter (transs-MIT-ur)—a device that sends out radio signals

venomous (VEN-uh-muss)—able to produce a toxic substance

vertebrate (VUR-tuh-bruht)—an animal that has a backbone

READ MORE

De Medeiros, James. *Anacondas*. Amazing Animals. New York: Weigl Publishers, 2009.

Ganeri, Anita. *Anaconda*. A Day in the Life: Rainforest Animals. Chicago: Heinemann Library, 2011.

Gray, Maurice. *Constrictors*. Animals Attack. Farmington Hills, Mich.: KidHaven Press, 2006.

INTERNET SITES

FactHound offers a safe, fun way to find Internet sites related to this book. All of the sites on FactHound have been researched by our staff.

Here's all you do:

Visit *www.facthound.com*

Type in this code: 9781429654326

INDEX

birth of, 20, 21
boas, 6, 14, 15
body temperature, 7, 21
Boidae family, 14

camouflage, 17
colors, 17, 18, 19, 26
constriction, 5, 8

feeding, 5, 8, 10, 11, 21

habitats, 7, 15, 16, 24, 27, 28
history, 6
hunting, 5, 8, 21, 23

Jacobson's organ, 10
jaws, 10, 26

lifespan, 22

mating, 20
myths, 10

name, 15

pelvis, 6
poachers, 28
predators, 21, 22
prey, 4, 5, 8, 10, 11
pythons, 6, 12, 14

Rivas, Jesús, 26–27

scales, 17, 26
size, 12–13, 18, 21, 22, 26, 28
skin, 10
species,
    Bolivian, 18, 19
    DeSchauensee's, 18, 19
    green, 16–17, 18
    yellow, 18, 19
spurs, 6
study of, 24, 26, 27
swallowing, 5, 8
swimming, 15

tails, 17
teeth, 5, 8, 23
tongues, 10
transmitters, 24

Venezuelan Wildlife
    Department, 24

weight, 13, 15, 16, 21
Wildlife Conservation
    Society, 24